LUCIFER SA. _

Peter Oswald

LUCIFER SAVED

OBERON BOOKS
LONDON

First published in 2007 by Oberon Books Ltd
521 Caledonian Road, London N7 9RH
Tel: 020 7607 3637 / Fax: 020 7607 3629
info@oberonbooks.com
www.oberonbooks.com

A catalogue record for this book is available from the British Library.

ISBN: 978 1 84002 807 2

Cover image: Oberon Books

Preface

The verse play *Lucifer Saved* was begun in reaction to an incident that took place in 1983. One of the Governors of Winchester College addressed an assembly of the entire school, to inform us of his innocence of a war crime charge. Finding him guilty, I set about thinking up a play about someone in his position committing such a crime and covering it up. He incriminates a crippled army Chaplain called Lucian Willow.

Peter Oswald
2007

Characters in the Play

LUCIAN WILLOW
an ex-army chaplain

LORD BROOK
an ex-colonel

SARAH
his daughter

MARGARET
his old nurse

WULF
a young German man

CLARA
a bearded woman

REGINALDA
a circus owner and clown

RONALDO
a contortionist and clown

CORPORAL BUCKLEY & PRIVATE WILLIAMS
ghosts

The play needs a cast of seven actors.
It's set in England in 1965.

Lucifer Saved was first performed on 30 October 2007 at the Finborough Theatre, London, with the following company:

LUCIAN WILLOW, Jacob Krichefski
LORD BROOK, Richard Franklin
SARAH, Liana Weafer
MARGARET / CLARA, Penelope Dimond
WULF, Pericles Snowdon
REGINALDA / CORPORAL BUCKLEY, Ria Jones
RONALDO / PRIVATE WILLIAMS, Tom Sangster

Directed by Reuben Grove
Designed by Louie Whitemore
Lighting by Scott McMullin
Music by Alastair Putt

Lucifer Saved was developed with Heart's Tongue Theatre Company, a Devon-based theatre company co-founded by Peter Oswald and Josephine Larsen.

SCENE ONE

LORD BROOK's house in Norfolk. Enter MARGARET carrying a tray of tea-things. Enter LUCIAN, walking. She sees him, screams, and drops the tea-things. LUCIAN falls to his knees and crawls off the other way.

SCENE TWO

Enter BROOK in great anxiety.

BROOK: Walking? That is impossible! A daydream!
    I told him only yesterday, that function
    Is gone from him, shall not come back again
    Till Cromwell shudders on his plinth, jumps down,
    And runs to crack the statue of the king
    With his bronze fist. So, are the cemeteries
    Safe? Can stone still weigh down the dead, bad dreams
    Still be contained inside the night's lead coffin?

Enter MARGARET.

Walking? You swear, Margaret?

MARGARET: Plain as my face. I screamed.

BROOK: So you said.

MARGARET: I blanched, Lord Brook. It was like a revenation. I had to slap myself to remember he is not dead, merely crippled; and yet, if cripples shall walk for no reason, it is no less terrifying, I maintain, as if the dead shall rise. It is a question of explanations. Let there be never such a controversy, I will listen patiently to the debate, and weigh up both sides, and choose neither – two reasons are better than none, but no reason is the abysm.

BROOK: Yes it is. Oh Margaret, what are we to do with him?

MARGARET: He is wheeling himself to and fro as gloomy as ever now as if nothing had happened, and I said to him, 'Will you be going for another walk later on, reverend?'

BROOK: Did you, did you, Margaret? And what did he answer you?

MARGARET: He looked at me as blankly as if I had asked the question in Persian. No – more blankly than that – as blankly as – I don't know how blankly, my dear, with a kind of wild and animal blankness such as you find only among the creatures of the profound deep who live in perpetual darkness.

BROOK suddenly collapses.

Oh your Lordship! Where is that teapot? Here's a cushion under your head! Oh! Cold! Wrap you up in this blanket! Hot sweet tea!

She rushes off and returns with hot sweet tea which she feeds to him in sips.

Can you speak? Can you speak? Shall I fetch the doctor?

BROOK: I did not think death would be like this – ushered
Out of life's courtroom by uncouth policemen,
When I had thought I was at least a witness,
If not the judge himself. I am condemned
For negligible crimes to endless crumbling!

MARGARET: What is it? What is it? I would never have guessed you would come to this, you were such a tough boy!

BROOK: Though I have not surrendered yet, thick gloom
Has seeped in through the wrinkles of my skin,
Filling the fagend of my life with anger!

MARGARET: What has made you so sad? What has made you so anxious? It is to do with him, isn't it? He walks, you fall down. What is it about him?

BROOK: That is not something you could understand
Dear Margaret. So you must not speak about him,
Or I will die right here in your thin arms,
And it will be your fault, you sweet old bittern.

MARGARET: Alright then! Let him remain mysterious, as most things are to the uneducated. But I will not stand by and see you wither, my promising boy; it is not an option. I will ice his birthday cake with arsenic, I will introduce big cats into his bedroom, if it will set you free from whatever this is! He is not even a member of the family, he is an alien, a foreign body, like a virus in the bloodstream. You are not so old yet, my little one; you are younger than me.

BROOK: I asked you not to speak about him!

MARGARET: Very well, he has dissolved on the tip of my tongue with a fizz, he is gone! And I will not even talk about murdering him. So what would make you happy then? What would make you young, my dream? I cannot raise the dead but –

BROOK: Oh leave them! What good did they ever do anyone? Beautiful though they may be. Leave them.

MARGARET: Something – some happy memory I could rekindle, some old tune I could pop on the gramophone. Apart from – with the dead – were you ever happy? Would you like to go to the theatre?

BROOK: Oh God!

MARGARET: The seaside?

BROOK: It has disappeared.

MARGARET: Scotland?

BROOK: A happy land?

MARGARET: The circus?

BROOK: Ha!

MARGARET: The circus?

BROOK: Well –

MARGARET: The circus! Come on!

BROOK: No. I cannot leave Brookleaze.

MARGARET: Why not?

BROOK: I cannot!

MARGARET: Why not?

BROOK: I do not want to – I do not want to die at any other address than my own!

MARGARET: You are not going to die!

BROOK: Oh yes I am.

MARGARET: Well bring the circus here then.

BROOK: Eh?

MARGARET: Bring it here! Bring it on! Invite a circus to Brookleaze and send out invitations to all the little Ipswich children to come with their mummies and daddies and fill the place with their tinselly laughter all at your expense and clamber on your knees with happy cries and you will be filled with their life and you will rejoice and be young again!

BROOK: Very well Margaret, I will do it! I will welcome onto my estate that simple, dedicated, disciplined, cold-eyed, hard-bodied, flexible tribe of performers!

Exeunt.

SCENE THREE

A circus truck driving through England. At the wheel, REGINALDA; next to her, CLARA and RONALDO. REGINALDA is swigging from a bottle of whisky and driving erratically at great speed.

REGINALDA: Ah England! Through your chimneys we descend,
Like smoke sucked back! You barrowful of weeds,
Heaped on the orange gleam of history,
That now and then a gust of poetry
Blows crimson! Oh my England, when oh when

Will a real wind come screaming from the sea
To spin your cocks, to make your faint sparks blossom
Into vermilion blooms of revolution!
Oh for a – give me the whisky would you, Ronaldo!

RONALDO: Yessir!

REGINALDA: How much further?

RONALDO: Three counties.

REGINALDA: I will eat up your shires!

RONALDO: There's a seventy mile an hour limit.

REGINALDA: You cannot limit me!

RONALDO: I'm talking about the law!

REGINALDA: How can you expect me to think about the law
when I am driving twenty tons of truck downwind through
England! Am I a judge? Am I a barrister? What case is this
before us? Am I competent to try it? I see a guilty country
spread out before me – I pass through it as quickly as I
can! I appeal to you, Clara! Tell me if I am wrong!

RONALDO: She's dumb!

REGINALDA: Her silence cries out in my cause, while you talk
about law!

RONALDO: You don't need to know the law to break the law!

REGINALDA: You don't need to know the law to break wind.
Am I right, Clara, darling? Say nothing if I am.

RONALDO: She's dumb!

REGINALDA: I know I am breaking every law ever invented,
my dear Ronaldo. I break them like sticks over my knee
and toss them into the fire!

RONALDO: Say this to the police!

REGINALDA: The law against floating. I hate that! The law against being adored by everyone. Why isn't there a law against law? I will not submit to this universal imprisonment, just because you say so, Ronaldo! Your interpretation of the law is not the only one!

RONALDO: I want to live!

REGINALDA: Why? What are your plans?

Exeunt at great speed.

SCENE FOUR

BROOK's house. Enter SARAH, wheeling LUCIAN.

SARAH: Then you led an army of Greeks into Persia and you conquered Persia! Don't you remember?

LUCIAN: No – I do not remember –

SARAH: Then you invented the telescope. Which got you into trouble with the Pope but – but you held it to your blind eye and said, I see no stars, and so you were not burnt.

LUCIAN: Was my eye blind once?

SARAH: Yes but you were healed.

LUCIAN: What happened next?

SARAH: After that you fell in love with a famous Frenchwoman – and her father, in her fury, had you castrated.

LUCIAN: Castrated?

SARAH: Yes castrated.

LUCIAN: That's bad.

SARAH: But a famous surgeon put you back together again.

LUCIAN: Oh thank God.

SARAH: And then you were the first man to walk on the moon.

LUCIAN: Good gracious!

SARAH: And you said –

LUCIAN: I said?

SARAH: You said –

> Twinkle twinkle little star
> How I wonder what you are,
> Up above the earth so high,
> Like a diamond in the sky.
> Twinkle twinkle little star,
> How I wonder what you are.

LUCIAN: Did I really say that?

SARAH: No.

LUCIAN: Is any of it true?

SARAH: No, Lucian. I'm sorry.

LUCIAN: Well you can tell me whatever you like!

SARAH: I know I can. But it's desperate! I'm sick of it! Look! A month ago you walked! Do you remember that?

LUCIAN: Yes.

SARAH: And what do you remember about it?

LUCIAN: The smell of freshly spilt tea on an old carpet.

SARAH: I was so excited, I thought, at last my only friend is turning back into himself! But nothing's changed.

LUCIAN: No.

SARAH: Do you not know what made you do it?

LUCIAN: I do know but –

SARAH: What? Tell me, tell me, Lucian!

LUCIAN: I do not know what I know.

SARAH: Do you accept, at least, that, logically speaking, your legs are legs, they do work?

LUCIAN: Yes, I accept that!

SARAH: And that therefore it is something in your head that is stopping them from walking.

LUCIAN: Or something in the past.

SARAH: Is there a difference?

LUCIAN: Well, my head is closer to me than the past is.

SARAH: I don't know about that. Well anyway we could not have spoken like this before you walked. So there has been a change. I am still almost excited about it! You do not know what you remembered, but you know that you remembered something. You know that your not being able to walk is a false proposition. You are fooling yourself, you know that.

LUCIAN: Yes.

SARAH: I almost think that you are ready to fend for yourself and that I could leave now, leave the sad old man and the cage full of birds and the birdwoman and the eternal topiary and go and find myself a friend with a memory. But no, it would be too unkind. And anyway where in the world would I find such an all-engrossing task as trying to remind you of something?

LUCIAN: You must leave, Sarah!

SARAH: Yes, Lucian, I must! But truly what will you do without me? He does not love you anymore!

LUCIAN: He never loved me!

SARAH: He does not like you anymore!

LUCIAN: He never liked me.

SARAH: Well – he is not even aware of you now – only of his own dying.

LUCIAN: It cannot come too soon.

SARAH: Oh do not say that, Lucian!

LUCIAN: My dear, you know that I have been your guardian since before the beginning of time!

SARAH: You have known me for six years.

LUCIAN: I have seen you not growing – under the shadow of that man – like a rose in the wrong place.

SARAH: You do not know anything – my empty friend!

LUCIAN: I know that it is not right. I have read in books. By now something should have changed, someone should have come to your rescue, or you should have escaped. Something always happens.

SARAH: Not to me.

LUCIAN: Well if you give me permission, my lady, I will make it happen. I will cut his throat with a shard of glass in the night, I will break his neck with a rope in the morning.

SARAH: Oh don't be ridiculous, Lucian. You have misread everything, outside the library you can't piece together what happens, it all goes by too quickly, you can't turn back the page. I am leaving today anyway, as it happens. I have only stayed on this long for you. But now that you say you want me to go, I will go. I do not know anything about the world, and you have not been able to tell me because you don't remember anything. I will just go and find my fortune on the streets of London, or somewhere – I think I might be a postwoman.

LUCIAN: Send me a letter!

SARAH: Here he is. I will tell him that I am going. Help me to stand my ground!

Enter BROOK.

BROOK: This is the great day! Sing out celebration!

Withdraw the rearguard of despair – the circus
Is coming! Jubilation, now my dying
Will be surrounded by the glee of children,
And I will exit as a child myself,
To death's new school! When I was young I loved
Circuses even more than stories, yearned
To run away and join one, be the boy
Who kept the camels, rise through the profession
To moustached man in leather boots who bellows!
But my inheritance would not unhitch me,
And I bowed low to my own birth, my title,
Lord Brook of Brook, myself, an outer coating
Soon to be washed off in the storm of dying!
But not today! Today the circus comes,
And I shall be immortal for a while.
Sarah, are you excited too?

SARAH: I am leaving.

BROOK: In protest at the circus?

SARAH: You did not tell me anything about it.

BROOK: Did I not?

SARAH: No.

BROOK: But I must have!

SARAH: When did you have the idea?

BROOK: Weeks ago!

SARAH: You have kept it very secret.

BROOK: I have been dreaming nothing else, my dearest.
How could I fail to speak to you about it?

SARAH: Well I am leaving.

BROOK: What are your intentions?

SARAH: To work.

BROOK: To work at what?

SARAH: Delivering.

BROOK: To be a midwife?

SARAH: No, a postwoman.

BROOK: Well I had hoped that you would like a circus.

SARAH: I am not six.

BROOK: I do not mean to watch it,
    But to be placed in care of the performers,
    To oversee their needs, and keep them smiling,
    To speak to them and listen to their stories;
    Then when they leave, to run away with them,
    Perhaps, but not before that! Give me notice,
    Sarah! This is the most amazing day
    Of my whole life – of my old age, for certain –
    The house is not the house, the fields around us,
    Not grass, but acres of anticipation
    Put in the place of what had grown as common
    As dandelions! Do not leave me laughing,
    Sarah my dear, at least let your leave-taking
    Be at a time when I can break down crying.
    I wanted you to share the celebration,
    And see me happy! I am very sorry
    That I forgot to tell you. I am fading,
    Falling apart. The plan is this – to offer
    Free tickets to the circus to all-comers!
    It is an inspiration sent from heaven,
    I think.

SARAH: The time has come. I must be going.

BROOK: They will be here in half an hour!

SARAH: Alright then!

Exit SARAH.

BROOK: Whisky?

LUCIAN: Thanks.

BROOK: Sleeping alright?

LUCIAN: Fine.

BROOK: No bad dreams?

LUCIAN: Not that I remember.

BROOK: But do you remember anything?

LUCIAN: What kind of things?

BROOK: Oh nothing. Well it looks like that was a bit of a false alarm then.

LUCIAN: What was?

BROOK: You walking.

LUCIAN: Oh well – I did remember something – then.

BROOK: You remembered something?

LUCIAN: I mean – something came into my mind.

BROOK: What kind of thing?

LUCIAN: Well it is so preposterous!

BROOK: How would you know what is and is not preposterous?

LUCIAN: It seems preposterous to me. God, if anything is preposterous, that is. If that is not preposterous, nothing is preposterous, and the word should simply be struck off, thrown out on the street!

BROOK: I wish you would explain exactly what you mean.

LUCIAN: Allow me to not. For the sake of grace. Let me at least believe that something is preposterous.

BROOK: I need to know!

LUCIAN: How do you know you need to know?

BROOK: I am looking after you!

LUCIAN: Why is that?

BROOK: Well Lucian, I will try to get it out of you. You know, you and I go back a long way.

LUCIAN: Do we?

BROOK: There is no one else alive I have known as long as I have known you. You and I have been through – great and terrible things! All the things that make me what I am, that grind my insides as if I had eaten a motorbike. It is a singular position to be in. Rearguard of all my companions, who have crossed over into nothing, I remain, dug in, and beside me, my best friend who scarcely remembers my name!

LUCIAN: Was I your best friend?

BROOK: Well anyway that is my memory. And there is no one left to dispute the point.

LUCIAN: How did we meet?

BROOK: You were the chaplain of my regiment. I see you are still nonplussed. Would you like me to explain from the beginning?

LUCIAN: Yes.

BROOK: God made man.

LUCIAN: Alright.

BROOK: And woman. So there were two. And they had two sons.

LUCIAN: Very good.

BROOK: One son killed the other son.

LUCIAN: I am sorry to hear it.

BROOK: A short leap later, after a series of revenges, Germany invaded France, not for the first time!

LUCIAN: France! Why?

BROOK: To pre-empt reprisals for their earlier invasions. And
you and I formed part of the Imperial Army of Britain, our
task to save these shores. Well that was my task. Your task
was to bury the dead and convince the living of eternal life
after the ceremony was ended. And you were my friend.

LUCIAN: What happened next?

BROOK: We fought the enemy in Africa. You must try to
provide the details with your imagination, my words are
bare wire, you must hang the dead bodies of young men
from them, you must provide the punctuation of guns. I
made errors, men died, you absolved me. You were my
friend.

LUCIAN: What happened then?

BROOK: We pursued our enemy to Italy. He was feeding
civilians into ovens. We responded with bombs dropped
from aeroplanes on his old mother stirring shoe soup in the
kitchen. You must place underneath my words, submarine
craft sinking ships full of children, the entire country of
Russia spasming in slaughter, Asia tortured. Yes the world
was like a man who thinks he has a cake of soap in his
hands, but it is a razor blade with which he is lathering.

LUCIAN: What happened in the end?

BROOK: In the end we took Berlin. Then there was a second
end. A man split the Adam, and chaos resumed, otherwise
known as peacetime. But you and I came to a full stop
in the capital city of the Germans, now divided between
four different nations. And it is in this place, truly, that we
begin. Yes in this place, truly, we can begin to understand
where we are standing, under what king we sit, cold Lords
of oblivion. Now we sense the dimensions of our cell
– steel sky, steel earth, steel walls of steel wind blowing
cold, with an unchanging sound. We sit very still. There
is a particular, thin, crooked moon smelling of lemon. A

blasted tree, hung with clothes for some reason. Berlin.
We are in Berlin. The small birds of May are singing their
tunes. The men are exhausted, with exasperated hands.
The women move rapidly in lines, not quite starving.
There has been a political collapse in heaven.

LUCIAN: And did I help you then?

BROOK: No. It was here that you deserted me, Lucian.

LUCIAN: What did I do?

BROOK: You did then something – for which I and the world
have forgiven you but which your mind cannot bear to
remember. And I will not state it in plain words. There
are no words plain enough to state it! It is for you to
remember!

Try man! I command you to remember! Remember!

LUCIAN: I am trying! I am trying!

BROOK: I think you are lying to me! For the first time I think
that you are lying! Well you will not crush me anymore!
Not anymore! The circus is coming!

Exit.

LUCIAN: Could it be true that he was once my friend,
That I stepped proud and honoured at his side,
Almost his equal, as the daystar shines
Close by retreating Venus in the morning?
Frank rows of buttons blazing on the green
Of my pressed surface, and between my eyes,
Where you might think that my third eye might be –
Cap button. He and I have been transformed
So strangely by the tampering of time,
We were two pillars keeping up the sky,
Now he is stooped, and I am permanently
Seated. We were companions, mingled streams,
Most intellectual friends. On me he leaned,
And pressed me almost into folded stone.

Now he is more my jailer than my ally,
Stiff broom that frightens spider thoughts of mine,
So that they scurry, leaving just the brain,
Dustily struggling in his draughty questions.
Since my friend Sarah will be leaving me,
What is it now that I must try to be,
And testily remember, chafing chin
To bone? I was a chaplain and his friend,
A man of God, and good. Then I did something
As vile and foul as I before had been
Shining and strong. He spoke about desertion.
That does not fit with what I have remembered,
But what I have remembered is obscene,
A sketch of chaos, fit to be discarded!
He would not say how I deserted him;
What did I do? By what almighty crime
Was I transduced from that man's sacred friend
To this diminished fifth, and how was he,
The dear companion of a holy man,
Reduced to crying out for death to end him?
He did not love a thing without a mind,
That could not even creep! By what declension
Am I a trumpet that will not resound?
Ah, now I see it, rising from the steam
At the world's end, I see my ghostly crime
Like a dead god, head vaster than the sky,
One eye the sun, the other eye the moon.
What is your name? Tell me, what is your name?

Exit.

SCENE FIVE

The gardens. Enter REGINALDA, RONALDO, CLARA.

REGINALDA: Where is this Lord? Where is this field? Where?
Sit down my darling. She is not happy here. Though there
is a kind of happiness in her unhappiness, like a man about
to be hanged who suddenly thinks, well I've done with all
that mopping and swapping, all that sweating and fretting,

swabbing and sobbing, leaking and shrieking, all that oozing and schmoozing and lying and frying and thinking and stinking and talking endless pointless crap!

RONALDO: That's enough, Reginalda!

REGINALDA: Stop my mouth with the bottle. Look, I have not yet detached myself from my vehicle, we're umbilically combined, my suspension is trembling, my oil's ready to burn. Sit me down, sit me down, do something to make me human. Put a checked cloth on the ground and spread it with triangles of cheese and squares of ham and we will send a geometrical meal down to the mess of our intestines. Baby tomato, darling?

RONALDO: We have nothing.

REGINALDA: Then let's feast on each other. Tell me about yourself, Ronaldo! This whisky is made from my own desalinated tears for all the small creatures I have trampled with my feet. Feet I have not seen for sixteen years. Feet that in my drunken prancing have killed cats, goats, old women.

RONALDO: Drink!

REGINALDA: Where is this Lord of old England who has invited us to set up our tent in his grounds and recover him from the worst bad mood since Fourteen Sixty-Nine?

Sings.

Far away
Where the chuckling children of the nightjar play
And the dusty sun sits waiting for the day
Far away
Where the earth turns in her yellow sleep to pray
For the icy bridegown as it slips away
Far away
Where the empty west has nothing left to pay
For the tinker's wedding of the milky way
Or so they say

Far away
Where the east is yet to fling its faintest ray
Still refusing to decline from black to grey
Far away
Far away
Far away
Far away

(*Speaks to* CLARA.) Do not be sad my darling, we have only set one foot on the ground. We can leap away at any instant, if they do not honour us. Though we have never trespassed on one another's flesh, your thoughts are entwined in mine. I will do all the talking, no need to stir. Oh but when she speaks, when that day comes, oh Lord! Haha! As the universe was created by God's soliloquoy, so shall it be undone when Madam Clara speaks her mind!

RONALDO: Let's hope it never happens. Ah, here's someone!

Enter SARAH.

SARAH: Are you the circus?

RONALDO: We are some of it.

SARAH: I am Sarah Brook.

RONALDO: Ah, your ladyship!

SARAH: I'm supposed to look after you. I don't know where my father is.

REGINALDA: Sadly so many are in the same plight.

SARAH: Probably in his office.

REGINALDA: Let's hope he comes out alive.

SARAH: What?

RONALDO: This is Reginalda Chichester, the owner of the circus. And this is Madam Clara. Your ladyship, would you be able to direct us to the correct field in which to set up our tent, or would you rather wait for your father to direct us?

SARAH: I think I know the field. That one, with the collapsed barn in the corner. But it would be best if you wait for my father to confirm it.

REGINALDA: This is a truly splendid place.

SARAH: Do you think?

REGINALDA: It is so lovely, with its fields and little woods, its humble animals sheltering in their half-ruined, half-timber buildings. And the garden! Paradise without nakedness, except in stone – and the big cage of birds, and the inconsolable fountains.

SARAH: This is where I was born.

REGINALDA: You must never leave!

SARAH: Ha!

REGINALDA: Heaven is irrelevant to one who was born in this place. Don't ever set foot in a church!

SARAH: I'll do what I want.

RONALDO: Is your father as depressed as you?

SARAH: I am not depressed.

REGINALDA: What a truly splendid state to be in! Not depressed! You do not know how lucky you are! The angels in heaven are not depressed! Rejoice! Hallelluia!

SARAH: You're to be a free show, did you know that? My father is paying for everyone.

REGINALDA: That really is truly truly quaint, isn't it?

SARAH: It's demented.

REGINALDA: And will you keep up the tradition after his death?

SARAH: No.

REGINALDA: Well I really am very depressed now.

SARAH: Oh! Here comes my father!

Enter BROOK.

BROOK: Aha! Reginalda Chichester, I believe!

REGINALDA: The same!

BROOK: Welcome, welcome everyone!

SARAH: This is Ronaldo.

BROOK: And what do you do?

RONALDO: Mostly I lift things.

BROOK: Good, good, only way to see what's under 'em! Dear God, don't I know you?

RONALDO: Yes you do, sir.

BROOK: Aren't you the – aren't you – the Switzer?

RONALDO: I was, sir!

BROOK: Good God, man! It does me good to see you! What was your name?

RONALDO: I am Ronaldo now, sir.

BROOK: Have you become Italian?

RONALDO: I have become a circus person.

BROOK: Deadliest sniper I have ever seen. Kept an entire Kraut Regiment pinned down single-handed near Monte Cassino. Hiding in a cave in a mountain – a network of caves – artillery demolished the entire mountain – this man emerges from a little crack in the ground, having survived on bat's droppings. What was your name?

RONALDO: Would you like to see a double back flip?

BROOK: Utterly fearless individual. Send him out at midnight with a length of cheesewire, reports back at dawn – the brigade may proceed, sir, in marching order.

RONALDO: Look – now I can do the spider!

BROOK: Comfort to have you around. Quells all fear of invasion!

He pats RONALDO on the back. RONALDO springs to attention.

REGINALDA: Not so bendy now.

BROOK: A steel wall, proof to all missiles.

REGINALDA: Ronaldo, are you stuck?

CLARA clicks her fingers. RONALDO collapses to the floor, slowly picks himself up.

SARAH: And this is Madam Clara.

BROOK: The bearded woman! Good heavens! Are you married?

REGINALDA: I must answer that question for her. Not yet. And nor will she be, until she finds a man like her father.

BROOK: What do you mean?

REGINALDA: Her mother was also bearded.

BROOK: Oh!

REGINALDA: And oh she was difficult to win! She did not believe his love for her! But at last he prevailed. And she died believing she was beautiful. There is someone for our Clara here, somewhere in this infinite life he is looking for her!

BROOK: Tell me more about her!

REGINALDA: She has second, third, fourth, fifth and sixth sight. She prophesied all my marriages. I said, can you see me marrying Alan? And she silently assented. Then I said, what about Neil? Again, she said nothing against it. And Mike and Stan and Tommy? No, she would never deny me, and now I have nine husbands, some clever, some not so clever.

BROOK: Madam – I must remark – this blaze of fur
Upon your face, this gentle auburn blur,
Uncommon in a woman, I concur,
That should provoke surprise or even fear,
Ruins your beauty and your grace no more
Than russet bracken on a snow-clad moor,
Or a small hazel island in a mere
Of brightest green. Your radiance, therefore,
I must conclude, spreads from an inward sphere,
Buried as deep as this blue earth's red core.

REGINALDA: She thinks you are terribly sensitive.

BROOK: Well I am an Englishman! And where are the rest of you? How are they?

RONALDO: Well the trapezist's dropped his girlfriend, the knifethrower's wife has stabbed him in the back, and someone's shot the human cannonball.

BROOK: I beg your pardon?

REGINALDA: Ronaldo! I am the clown!

BROOK: And have you always been a clown?

REGINALDA: I was born into it. My grandfather was a pratt, and my father was a blithering idiot. I learned everything from them, and turned what I learned into the skill I now possess for the benefit of everyone!

BROOK: How long has your circus been going?

REGINALDA: It was eternal for a number of years, and then the Churchill-Hitler spat caused a long intermission – yes – the flying Cunninghams, shot down defending Malta, Ralph and Olly, our clowns, captured on special operations and hanged. Our elephants, our knife-thrower, our performing horses, all commandeered for military purposes and thrown away for nothing – well, I mean, not for nothing, we won the war or shall we say a lengthy stalemate has been caused – but after all that I vowed that once more carousels would turn and that ladies with small breasts would hang from ropes by their teeth. So I bought myself a comedy collapsing car and set off across Europe in search of – performers!

BROOK: Fascinating! Well we have met! Everything I own is yours, help yourselves to all you need of earth air water and fire! Let me show you to the patch of sky I wish you to fill with your billowing canvas. This way!

Exeunt all but SARAH.

SARAH: (*Sarcastically.*)
Why should I not be happy in this place,
A simple country virgin, pale of face,
With rooted thoughts that in their seasons bud
And scatter their red petals in the mud?
As I stand green and weeping like a tree,
Behold the whole wide weird world comes to me!

Enter LUCIAN.

LUCIAN: My lady, may I engage you in conversation?

SARAH: Speak on.

LUCIAN: I apologise for my earlier confusion. I realize now how absurd it was for me to speak of cutting out your father's throat with a shard of glass or yanking off his head with a cow-rope. I do not wish to endanger our friendship. I am, as you say, an empty vessel, making hollow sounds. That is why I am here, in this beautiful and quiet place where you and your father, out of kindness, keep me.

SARAH: I accept your apology. You weren't far wrong, anyway.

LUCIAN: I also wish to apologise for implying that anything could be wrong between yourself and your father. He is a sad man, of course, he misses your mother, who died when you were born. He has never remarried. You have had to carry his lack, plug that great gulf no amount of beef or beer could ever make good. You and he are extraordinarily close. One would need an electron microscope to pinpoint the slightest gap! A man like me, an outsider, could never have the tiniest hope of ever detecting the encyclopaedia of feeling you each express to the other with a mere word or flinch. I am a fool! I am a trespassing goat, and deserve to be tied with dangling saucepans and set loose in the wilderness! You will not leave this place! You are this place! And this place is your father's heart! All is right, nothing's amiss!

SARAH: No, Lucian, you were right. I hate. I want to – out – but he got round me again.

LUCIAN: How does he do it?

SARAH: It is nothing that he does. But always something happens.

LUCIAN: Magic!

SARAH: No doubt.

LUCIAN: Certainly he speaks to me in mysterious ways.

SARAH: What has he said?

LUCIAN: He has once again attempted to remind me of former times.

SARAH: Oh yes!

LUCIAN: The dangers we shared – and my prayers!

SARAH: But you have not remembered?

LUCIAN: It is as if there is something that remains unsaid.

SARAH: How far did he get?

LUCIAN: To the end. So I thought. To Berlin. And then – it is as if after that something happened. Something strange.

SARAH: Well yes.

LUCIAN: Ah! He has spoken to you about this then?

SARAH: Yes!

LUCIAN: It is almost as if I were to ask you – what is it that I did?

SARAH: I cannot tell you that.

LUCIAN: No of course not.

SARAH: You would not thank me. And anyway, I can't talk about it! When you remember of your own accord – alright. But it would not be fair to speak before that. You are innocent!

LUCIAN: No I am not.

SARAH: Yes! At this moment you are innocent.

LUCIAN: No I am not. No I am not.

SARAH: Up goes the tent!

LUCIAN: Like a brassiered bosom in a seaside postcard!

SARAH: And the flag snapping in the wind like a dog on a lead.

LUCIAN: A Skye terrier.

SARAH: It is wonderful, the things you do remember –

Enter REGINALDA, CLARA, RONALDO.

REGINALDA: Well that's the build up.

SARAH: I beg your pardon?

REGINALDA: We call putting up the tent, the build up, your Majesty. Pulling it down we call the pull down. Moving it from place to place we call the pull through.

SARAH: How fascinating.

REGINALDA: Not as fascinating as your own guts hanging out.

SARAH: This is Lucian Willow.

LUCIAN is staring at CLARA.

REGINALDA: Have you seen her before?

LUCIAN: No. Forgive me. Perhaps in a dream.

REGINALDA: Forgive me!

LUCIAN: For what?

REGINALDA: For any offence I may cause through not knowing you, and for letting you down if we ever become friends. May I present you with this, my lady?

She hands her a shrunken skull.

I have carried it through the world since I was a girl, hoping to find the one maiden to whom it would be appropriate to pass it on. Not Genghis Khan's hanky, or anything special really, except to me. I was given it by an invisible woman – or so she became shortly after we met. It belonged to Robinson Crusoe. Not exactly Robinson, but a man who was lost on a desert island – no one knows his name – sadly the inhabitants ate him. We know of his life by the notebook he kept, containing several poems of which I quote one:

Alone, alone, oh, oh, alone,
Alone, alone, alone.
Alone, alone, oh, oh, alone,
Alone, alone, alone.
Alone.
Alone.
Alone.
Oh.
Oh.
Oh.
Oh.
Alone.
Alone, alone, alone, alone,
Alone, alone, alone.

It goes on like that for forty-five pages. To me there is nothing more lonely in this universe that is so crowded and packed with loneliness, than this little memento of a man with less than no luck, who ended up, not merely without friends to dine with, but dined on by the only company he could find. We must stand guard against the thought that such things never happen. There is always one step further down.

SARAH: Thank you.

REGINALDA: It has only one magical quality.

SARAH: Oh?

REGINALDA: That whatever happens to it, that fate is prophetic of the owner's. I have been anxious to get rid of it as auspiciously as I might, before an elephant treads on it, or it is made into a nest by mice. If you accept it, my future is extremely bright.

SARAH: So tempting to refuse.

REGINALDA: You could! You could!

RONALDO: She tried to give it to me.

REGINALDA: I did not!

SARAH: I don't care about that! I accept the gift.

RONALDO: I should give it to charity quick.

SARAH: You think I'm scared of it?

RONALDO: You should not have accepted it!

He pickpockets the skull.

REGINALDA: Now we are inextricably linked!

SARAH: No we're not.

REGINALDA: Madam, have you ever been in love?

SARAH: No.

REGINALDA: Ronaldo has stolen it!

SARAH: Ronaldo!

RONALDO: To spare you from a worse fate!

SARAH: I'm not scared of fate!

REGINALDA: You give it back!

RONALDO: I will not!

REGINALDA: You withered little stick! Strike him, your
    ladyship! Expel him from your estates! He is superfluous to
    our purposes!

SARAH: Please give it back!

REGINALDA: You winkled rock! You heap of unrecognisable
    refuse! Attention! Hands off cocks, on with socks! You're
    sacked!

RONALDO gives it back. REGINALDA beats him offstage.

SARAH: No fighting on the estate! Stop clowning about!

Exeunt all but LUCIAN. The skull is left lying on the ground.

LUCIAN: Willow is evil. He is who I am,
    I must be evil or I will disform,
    Unwreathe like mist, disintegrate, play dumb
    In someone else's story with no end;
    My friend remembers, I must honour him
    As prophet tablet, soldier fatherland,
    Though he has only told me I did wrong,
    Not what I did – but that is something, something!
    He tames with names all wild and disparate things,
    Foremost myself, a cliff of smoke to climb
    With hands of ash, till he proclaimed my doings,
    Now a firm platform in the marsh of nothing,
    Where like a mermaid I will tread, a scream
    At every step, across the too-hard ground,
    Preferring that to foamy dissipation;
    I shall not honour my own memory,

That pit of cess, but bow to his alone;
Willow is wicked, he must cheat and steal,
First taking this. And from this theft my friend
Receives a curse, or so I understand.

He puts the skull under his jacket and wheels off. Enter
REGINALDA, CLARA, SARAH, and RONALDO.

REGINALDA: Gone! Gone!

SARAH: This is the place where you gave it to me!

REGINALDA: Search every blade of grass!

RONALDO: It ought to stand out.

REGINALDA: What have you done with it?

RONALDO: I was with you all the time!

REGINALDA: Trust not the heart of a contortionist!

RONALDO: Don't try and unload your guilt!

REGINALDA: Guilt for what?

RONALDO: For giving such an onerous present!

REGINALDA: Onerous? Where have you hidden it?

RONALDO: I have not!

REGINALDA: Ah, you have burnt it!

RONALDO: This is all your fault!

REGINALDA: Beware! I am a far more imposing character than
you are!

RONALDO: But you are in the wrong!

REGINALDA: That's irrelevant!

SARAH: Don't fret. I'm not worried about it.

REGINALDA: But I am! Give it back!

RONALDO: I haven't got it!

REGINALDA: Get on your knees and swear that you didn't take it!

RONALDO: I will not!

REGINALDA: She is desperate!

RONALDO: No she isn't.

REGINALDA: Is there a single drop of human blood in your heart?

RONALDO: Yes.

REGINALDA: Then kneel and swear! To ease her mind at least! Then we can rule you out of our enquiries.

RONALDO: I might kneel and lie through my teeth. None of that swearing means anything to me.

REGINALDA: Ah! Clear as ice! This is the guilty man! Nothing means anything to him, not a young girl's hopes of happiness, on which the stars themselves depend for their glittering! Oh it's a dark world, a dark world you want for us! Kneel, kneel and pray for forgiveness, you have set your foot on the spring of all sweetness, from now on this world will be awash with the tears of torturers!

RONALDO: I did not steal the gift.

REGINALDA: He can twist his soul into any shape.

SARAH: I'm really not worried about it!

REGINALDA: Dear Christ, the girl's courage! It turns me into an autumn leaf! Yet there he stands, in the face of all fearlessness, and holds his silence! Go on, twist the knife!

RONALDO: I'm not saying anything.

REGINALDA: Go on, ply the lash! I should have left you in your sleepy Alpine village! He was a curate! If I had known the bitterness bubbling in his pancreas!

RONALDO kneels.

RONALDO: Alright! I swear I did not take it!

SARAH: I didn't think you did!

REGINALDA: Your vows mean nothing to us! You have
destroyed our faith! Get up, get up, you little Swiss creep!

RONALDO: Take that back!

REGINALDA: Yodleayehee! (*She yodles and imitates cowbells.*)

RONALDO: Very well, I am leaving!

REGINALDA: Oh don't go! You see the trouble with you is you
really can't take a tease! Now where's that skull?

Enter LUCIAN. The skull is visible poking just out of his jacket.

LUCIAN: What have you lost?

SARAH: The little skull Reginalda gave me.

LUCIAN: What? Already? But that means –

SARAH: I am already lost. If that's to be my future, well at least
I'm used to it.

LUCIAN: I just don't believe it! Where did you last see it?

REGINALDA spots it.

REGINALDA: Oh! Wait! I'm getting a vision of it!

LUCIAN: Oh good!

REGINALDA: It fades! It fades! No – it comes clear again! The
skull! The skull! Someone has got it under his jacket.

SARAH: I hope he hands it in to the house. Is it one of our
employees?

REGINALDA: No – a man out of work.

RONALDO: Is he looking for employment?

REGINALDA: He is content simply to sit.

RONALDO: What a lazy sod.

REGINALDA: He is right here among us!

Points to LUCIAN.

SARAH: Lucian! You've got it!

LUCIAN: I – what?

REGINALDA: The gift. It is under your jacket.

LUCIAN: Is it?

REGINALDA: Yes it is. Someone has stamped on it.

LUCIAN: Yes, now I remember, I was bringing it back!

SARAH: And you forgot – of course you did.

RONALDO: Never mind. Alright now. You can wash it.

REGINALDA: My lady, may I speak with you aside?

SARAH: You may.

REGINALDA: He stole it.

SARAH: I know. He probably did. He can't help it. We are
looking after him. He went mad in the war. My father gave
him a job in his bank and he stole so we brought him here.
He's my only friend, I'm used to him. He doesn't know
he's doing it.

REGINALDA: If this fellow is your only friend, my lady, then I
fear for you!

SARAH: He is a perfect saint compared to what he once was.
Who is that young man walking in the garden?

REGINALDA: I do not know. All I know is that we have been
too long on the loose. We must be practising!

Exeunt REGINALDA and RONALDO.

SARAH: Who is that person walking in the garden?

Exit. Only LUCIAN and CLARA remain.

LUCIAN: Madam, you more than pierced me with your eyes,
    Moving me to some sense of recollection.
    And you are doing it again, prospecting
    In my interior. There are no diamonds
    Fit to be found, in that exhausted mountain!
    Yet your eyes seem to reach up angel hands
    And set the Sunday bells of heaven swinging
    On a weekday, to warn of an invasion
    From hell. You stir the sediment of poison
    Long settled on the bottom of the cauldron,
    And it sends up sharp gimlets of green fumes
    That pierce straight through the sinus to the brain.
    I am remembering, remembering –
    Nothing! I have to be a Chaplain, Madam,
    That is the key – a man of fixed religion,
    But not a good man – no – by faith's pretension
    I paved a churchyard path to love's destruction,
    Made my friend hate me. In a former time,
    Now lost in – lost in – . It is not enough
    For me to simply be an unkind person,
    I must be stench pretending to be perfume,
    I must be outwardly the best of men,
    But inwardly, and in my truest actions,
    Horrible. Madam, that is what I am,
    No other facts about me have been passed down
    From the beforetimes, that heroic aeon
    When everything was clear and plain and open!
    I see that you are like myself, a person
    Who in the mirror of her mind sees nothing,
    When she looks into it. We are us, madam!
    You see I must be what they say I am.
    So let me sleep, and dream I am a chaplain.

He sleeps. She kisses him and leaves. Re-enter SARAH with WULF.

WULF: Is it the gracious daughter of the place?

SARAH: What? Yes. And who are you?

WULF: My name it is Wulf Tanner.

SARAH: What are you doing here?

WULF: I am from Germany come.

SARAH: What?

WULF: From Germany. Germania.
    This is the garden of Lord Brook, I take it?

SARAH: Yes.

WULF: How mighty are the trees!

SARAH: They are tall. Some of them.

WULF: How bright the grass!

SARAH: We have had quite a lot of rain.

WULF: And sky! As if sackful of smashed mirrors crammed
    into skull turn thought into light, reflection triply reflecting,
    infinitely bright, like eye in eye flashing!

SARAH: It is a clear day.

He gives her a letter. She looks at it.

So you are from my father's old regiment.

WULF: If it is yet a desert that I tread,
    Lady I know not. Still no compass point
    Fixes the swirl of space in which I drift,
    But I keep forward.

SARAH: Do you want to speak to my father?

WULF: Yes! Yes!

SARAH: Well he is – well – do not speak to him – I do not
    know where he is – also he is very old, very very old
    indeed, oh so old! Speak to me.

WULF: I see you are the Lady of the place.

SARAH: Well in a sense. What did you want to say?

WULF: As your great poet Spencer said – well I forget – never
    mind –

    Where is my father? But I fly too fast,
    Skip the whole island, land in emerald Ireland.
    And language is a net with mesh too fine
    For sense to slip through. From the deep it shooms,
    Froth-crackling with a catch too big to land!
    Normally I speak clearly but my nerves
    Jangle my English into something strange!

SARAH: Then take it slowly, Wulf, one thought at a time.

WULF: Thank you!

SARAH: It's fine.

WULF: First step – my birth. No, moving sprintly on –
    I with your father's regiment gain employment
    At age eighteen. My mother leaves me then,
    Since I was placed, like famous king on column,
    Lolly on stick. Liaison is my calling,
    Interpretation: as a go-between,
    To be a beacon of the Occupation
    To the pitch midnight of my countrymen,
    Fishing in oil with the unravelling
    Thread of their own suits! Hopeless occupation!
    But why so many images of fishing?
    My occupation was the Occupation:
    To make it shine for my blind countrymen.
    But that is by the by. I am, have been,
    Changed, by a typed, official revelation!

SARAH: Oh Wulf, tell me – steadily, steadily –

WULF: Lady, am is not not what might have been.
    And yet, it is.

SARAH: I think I understand.

WULF: Father is are – and so, by gleam and gleam –
    Forgive me my unmilitary mind!

According to report your father signed,
The same he filed in Nineteen Forty-Five,
Being the utmost year that I am born –
My father is a chaplain by the name
Lucian Willow, and – I cannot say
The means –

SARAH: I know them.

WULF: I, like sprat in spray,
Finding the ring the Princess cast away,
To then ingest it and, digesting, die!

SARAH: What did you say?

WULF: He then, as drenched in vodka by his crime,
Staggering through Berlin's senility,
Set foot on fate, that lofted him in blaze,
To soft him down as blank as newborn babe!

SARAH: You did not find this out – it found you.

WULF: As if a husband in a screaming stream
Of bomb-blast bloodied women, suddenly
Find himself blubbing in his own wife's arms!

SARAH: It is almost enough to make you believe – some small
thing.

WULF: Where is my father now? I know you say,
One crime is tiny – thus no doubt my mother,
Who never whistled snatch of this to me –
To question of my father answered she
Always with, war flick many such away
As it suck sighing on gold tipped sobranie,
Shuffling again. In my night-wondering,
He Bormann, no, he Himmler, Hitler he!
But no – a Chaplain in the British army!

SARAH: Ah Wulf!

WULF: And I fail burying that fact away.
So do I sail far-seeking over sea.

SARAH: You want to find your father. But when you do, what
    will you do to him?

WULF: Might as well ask the Sphinx the way to Thebes!
    I know and do not know – I cannot say –
    But I must see him, as the sky the day!

SARAH: Where is your mother now?

WULF: In mystery.

SARAH: Ah Wulf, so is mine.

WULF: Your meaning?

SARAH: When my father was in France, my mother was in
    London with another man. This was just after I was born.
    I was here, in the countryside. A buzzbomb hit the house
    she was in. She and her lover went up in smoke. Khakhi
    and lace were scattered for miles around, and a black
    question mark of smoke stood above Hampstead. My
    father was a laughing man, they say, before. But I have
    never seen any trace of that. My mother was a singer. But
    me – he will not let me sing.

WULF: Oh sing for me!

SARAH: What shall I sing?

WULF: Sing anything!

SARAH: (*Sings.*)
    Who would true valour see,
    Let him come hither!

WULF: Wonderful!

SARAH: No!

WULF: Encore! Encore! Please!

SARAH: Er –

    One here will constant be
    Come wind come weather!

There's no discouragement
Can make him once relent –

WULF: Beautiful, beautiful song!

SARAH: His first avowed intent
To be a pilgrim!

WULF: I cannot believe my ears! Heaven is open!

SARAH: My Bonnie lies over the ocean –

WULF: Yes!

SARAH: My Bonnie lies over the sea –

WULF: Aha!

SARAH: My Bonnie lies over the ocean –

WULF: What? Still?

SARAH: Oh bring back my Bonnie to me!

WULF: Bring her back!

SARAH: Bring back, bring back –

WULF: Please!

SARAH: Oh bring back my Bonnie to me,
To me,

WULF/SARAH: Bring back, bring back,
Oh bring back my Bonnie to me!

WULF: Hurrah!

SARAH: Oh thank you.

WULF: Now can you tell me where my father is?

SARAH: There. That is him.

WULF: What? Him? This fellow sleeping?
This cosy snoring warmth is Lucian?

SARAH: What will you do about him?

WULF: What is to do? I curse him! What does that mean?
Nothing! I have no wizard power in cursing! Yet what
shall I do? Tip him onto the ground? Petty dementure of
action, lacking meaning. Can I rage, like victim exultant
at execution, digesting death, a feast of nothing! Best I
could do would be against myself, his nearest – but no,
something he cares for! You perhaps! But that is nothing.
There is no room in the universe to fling him, no shame
foul enough to bury him under. Mind fails, ripping open
boxes of horror, only in the deepest night of a dream's
dream the fitting punishment hides, like Imperial diamond,
big as India, perfect indignity everlasting, infinity of
sobbing penitence spurned! Begetter of this filth of
flesh, and all the tears of my mother, all these eyes have
unwillingly seen, tired, sour, bitter country of my birth
engulfing me, shameful old people, venerable liars and
grizzled killers! My life of poison! I spit it back at you! You
are secure of murder, disappointment infinite that would
be, too swift, almost a gift, like these bones you have forced
me to carry, this air you cursed me to breathe! Creator of
hate, god of perpetual spite! In your heaven of forgetting
– which how have you earned?

SARAH: Wulf you are right, he still does not remember.

WULF: Well I will find my mother and she will make him
remember!

SARAH: He still will not! He is a nothing, Wulf. But do not
imagine that he is happy, he is like a sea with no fish, like
a world of snow with no footprints or marks of any kind,
and the wind that blows over that waste is sad, suffers, I am
sure, full of tears that do not fall. He has suffered as much
as you and I have done!

WULF: Is that certain?

SARAH: We should not be enemies, we are the three most
downtrodden beings that have ever been.

WULF: How strange we should meet!

SARAH: How strange!

They kiss.

Promise me one thing!

WULF: Anything!

SARAH: When he wakes, do not tell him who you are – not yet! He is beginning to remember – let it happen gently!

WULF: Well I have already promised.

They kiss again.

You will come with me to London! You know the world is all spring outside this place, people turning into daffodils – music, madness! Only this place not! Only this place death!

LUCIAN wakes up, singing.

LUCIAN: Who would true valour see,
Let him come hither!
One here will constant be,
Come wind come weather!
There's no discouragement
Can make him once relent
His first avowed intent
To be a pilgrim!

A hymn! A hymn! I have remembered a hymn!

WULF: Ah, so you have woken!

LUCIAN: Sarah! Sarah! I have remembered my religion!

SARAH: Have you? What else have you remembered?

LUCIAN: Nothing – nothing – nothing. But now I recall my vocation! I could take a service today – you may leave me, I can stand on my own two feet, I know what I am!

SARAH: You cannot stand!

LUCIAN: Yes I can!

He stands.

SARAH: This is amazing!

LUCIAN: I am awash with blessings! Get me a bishop! It has happened! I remember my prayers – dearly beloved, we are gathered here in the presence of – in the presence – in the presence of almighty God – it is all coming back to me! I am well-trained! You may leave me now forever, I can make my way! Who are you?

WULF: I am – Wulf Tanner.

LUCIAN: Welcome, welcome to the world, my son!

Enter BROOK, CLARA, REGINALDA, RONALDO.

SARAH: Lucian has remembered!

BROOK: My old friend!

LUCIAN: No, I have not remembered you, I have remembered myself only, I am sorry, old friend. I have been recaptured by my religion, the entire institution has reawoken inside me, I am a great cathedral full of singing, but it drowns out all other sounds.

REGINALDA: Reverend Willow has returned! I love you, Lucian, and Madam Clara loves you, and so does Ron, don't you Ron?

RONALDO: Well I mean I'm sure I will in time.

REGINALDA: He is descended from lizards. Love, love, love! It is a mammalian instinct, not known to cobras! For heaven's sake, Ron, can't you evolve a bit, just for the occasion?

CLARA weeps.

She weeps! See, she weeps! Tears sliding through her beard like slugs through moss! Put your ears to her head and you will hear heaven's bells!

SARAH: What will you do, Lucian?

BROOK: Let's not push him into anything. He is only just out of the cocoon. Let him sit in the sun till his wings dry. Who is this young man?

WULF: I am Wulf Tanner.

SARAH: This is Lord Brook, my father.

WULF: I am a friend of your daughter; Wulf Tanner.

BROOK: What? Where did you come from?

SARAH: I will explain –

BROOK: Do not ambush me with surprises!

SARAH: Calm down!

REGINALDA: Reverend Willow has awoken! Ring bells, tell heaven!

BROOK slaps RONALDO on the back again, who stands to attention. CLARA frees him again. He crawls off. Exeunt.

Interval or interlude of wurlitzer music.

SCENE SIX

Enter BROOK to the garden in great misery. Enter PRIVATE WILLIAMS and CORPORAL BUCKLEY, gardening, in military uniform.

BROOK: Who are you men?

WILLIAMS: We are your gardeners, sir.

BROOK: Why are you in uniform?

BUCKLEY: Force of habit, sir.

BROOK: Let me see your faces.

WILLIAMS: We're a handsome pair, we are.

BUCKLEY: Romeo's replicas.

BROOK: Williams? Private Williams?

WILLIAMS: The same!

BROOK: Corporal Buckley?

BUCKLEY: It is he, it is he!

BROOK: You are dead!

WILLIAMS: Yes sir!

BROOK: Then what are you doing in my garden?

BUCKLEY: We've mulched round the apple trees, sir, and separated some of the bulbs. We have transplanted a heap of Michaelmas daisies from the edge of the meadow to the top of the lawn here. We want it all nice for the wedding.

BROOK: Get out!

BUCKLEY: Ah, there be a deal of mowing yet to do, sir.

WILLIAMS: We won't leave till the place is a regular Eden, sir. But we must break at eleven.

BUCKLEY: Come on then Williams.

WILLIAMS: Righty-ho, Corporal Buckley. Have you got a speck of tobacco to spare?

BUCKLEY: Oh I should reckon.

Exeunt BUCKLEY and WILLIAMS. Enter WULF and SARAH.

SARAH: Good morning father!

BROOK: Is it really morning?

Exit.

SARAH: It is the morning of my wedding!

WULF: Truly I think our love he has forgotten!
It is too swift a growth and too all-changing,
Sets knife in place of fork, serves soup as pudding,
Removes all spoons. It is a revolution

So fast it changes even retrospection,
Makes Italy a colony of Holland,
India German! In the flower garden
Roe deer are rooted in the ground and blooming,
While in the greenwood the red rose is running!

SARAH: Is six months sudden?

WULF: From first kiss to wedding
It is quite quick. And I myself am qualmed –
Not about that, but I do have my question.

SARAH: What is your question?

WULF: Is Willow truly fit to take our wedding?
Six months is nothing for our love's foundation,
Indeed, but for the gentle reassembling
Of an entire mind – that must take much longer;
As planets out of fragments were cohered,
In the great spinning arc of burning gravel,
Over the process of ten billion years,
Not in an instant, so a human mind,
That can contain all this and more in daydreams,
Must take its tranquil time to form, like dome
Of porcelain cathedral, pieced by inches.

SARAH: He seems of sound mind.

WULF: Six months ago he did not know God's name!

SARAH: But he has caught up quick!

WULF: Yet there is still such schism in his thinking,
Between the dark and light, between what can
And what cannot be summoned. And I find,
It is a kind of curate's egg, his mind,
Platypus, mermaid, magpie, Anglican,
Not this or that. You know he was best friend
Of your poor father, but does not remember
All that, nor any military tie,
But only porches, altars, spires and naves,
As if one half his life was cast away

Into the sleeping sea, and we know why!
And I would like to tell him of his crime,
So he and I can speak about that theme,
With shared intelligence and equal footing.
Yes I would like to fill the spaces in,
Yes I would like to give him back his mind.
But you forbid that.

SARAH: Yes Wulf, I forbid that! At some point, yes, but not yet!
He is only just beginning to peep above the ground, let
him progress, do not run to stamp on him! Our marriage
will be his first service for more than twenty years! He will
be much stronger after that. Then we can begin to open
some of the truth to him so that he can repent and be
properly forgiven. Then he will be your father and you will
be his son. As for my father and I, today is the tombstone
of our last chance. On this day my wounds are thrown
wide open, ready to be healed or worsened by what he
does or does not do or say. And since you came, he has
changed into a speared whale. Time is running out like blood.

WULF: It does not matter. Look, my little darling,
Only one single thing has ever happened –
From the beginning it has been unfolding –
Now it is happening to us; the stream
That drives the world's wheel in its sparkling circle,
Is us, my darling. Father did command
Silence, but father is a shifting wind,
Today a block of speaking steel, tommorrow
Dead leaves and feathers. Only we are rising
Into the light!

SARAH: We are. But it is tragic.

Enter LUCIAN.

LUCIAN: My happy couple!

SARAH: How are you feeling?

LUCIAN: Me? Fine! Sound of wind and limb!

WULF: No nightmares?

LUCIAN: Nothing!

WULF: Wonderful!

LUCIAN: The bishop is completely confident. He phoned me
first thing, said, full steam ahead, do the wedding, have no
fear, you and the happy couple will emerge victorious!

WULF: Hurrah!

LUCIAN: I thank you and I thank you and I thank you, you
lovely people, for being my guinea pigs!

WULF: It is you that are the pig!

LUCIAN: In a sense yes! I am the experiment. I am the mouse
in the maze. But you are the cheese, I guess!

WULF: The happy cheese!

LUCIAN: Yes! I am just going to have a last look at my notes.

SARAH: Alright!

Exit LUCIAN.

WULF: Thank you, father!

SARAH: Hush, Wulf, hush my darling.

Exeunt. Re-enter LUCIAN with CLARA.

LUCIAN: So now I am a Chaplain once again,
Only one thing remains for me to learn –
What did I do!? If I can glean that crime
From the drenched cornfield of the world's wrongdoings –
Extasy! Every petty criminal
Raging against the prosecution's cunning,
Is richer in the mind than I am; rolling
In mental treasures while I count out nothing;
I am stripped bare, truth does not cling to me,
I lack the central fact! And I will welcome
Any foul beast smeared with that information,

Into my heart, that stable is too clean!
Better a mansion where a monster groans,
Than one unused, whose ceiling is collapsing.
Madam, that is a truth I know for certain.
And so do you. As for the memory
That made me walk the first time, I have crammed
That laughing corpse into a compost bin,
And we will hear no more about it, madam,
It is forgotten! It is not forgotten;
But it will be forgotten – it is rotting!

Exit CLARA.

That is not how a vicar should speak. She leaves me,
and I am Lucian again. But in her presence I am – as it
were, words scratched into the stone of a tomb, crying
out helplessly through moss a too-brief and weathered
description of a different time, inexplicable to those who
peer now and, fingering me, hope at least to trace my
name and date! What is it? Not love. Not memory – we
have never met! What then? But she has left now, the
green smoke has drifted out of me, I am clear again and I
am present and I am Lucian.

Exit. Enter BROOK with MARGARET.

MARGARET: Why are you so down in the dumps? The circus
didn't do much good, did it? Well it did for a while, you
liked the fire-eater, didn't you?! That made you smile. And
they've all become friends of the family and they're all
here for the wedding and –

BROOK collapses.

Oh my goodness! What is it?

BROOK: Margaret, this marriage must not happen!

MARGARET: Why not? Wulf's a nice boy isn't he? It's not his
fault he's German. Anyway we can forgive and forget, can't
we? What's a few million dead and a few cities bombed?
Anyway it wasn't him, was it? He's too young. I think we

can forgive him. And if his dad's a Nazi, well for heaven's sake, a wedding's only one day, you won't have to have him for christmas. Or are you sad cos you're losing your little one?

BROOK: You have never seen into my heart!

MARGARET: Well that's not entirely my fault, is it? That organ is defended like the crown jewels. The moon is easier to reach. But I have tried, I have given my life to the endeavour, and who knows, before you die, my footprints may be seen on the dusty surface of that wobbling object.

BROOK: Margaret, there is something you don't know –

MARGARET: Most things fall into that category.

BROOK: It's horrible!

MARGARET: What is?

BROOK: Oh Margaret! Wulf is Lucian's son!

MARGARET: What? How do you know?

BROOK: Wulf told me. But we have not told Lucian.

MARGARET: Why not?

BROOK: I forbid it! I forbade Wulf!

MARGARET: Why?

BROOK: Because if Lucian – oh Margaret, it isn't true!

MARGARET: What isn't true?

BROOK: (*Genuinely surprised.*) What did you say?

MARGARET: I said, What isn't true?

BROOK: I don't know. Did I say something wasn't true? I do not think I said that. Everything is true.

MARGARET: Everything?

BROOK: Oh Margaret!

MARGARET: Speak! Open up, you big baby!

BROOK: I can't!

MARGARET: Oh God!

BROOK: Margaret, all I can tell you is that this wedding must be stopped, it cannot happen, yet to stop it now, somehow to wreck it, would be abomination!

MARGARET: Well I can't say anything. You won't tell me why it can't happen. Can't a Vicar marry his own son?

BROOK: Margaret!

MARGARET: Get up, get up. If you must wreck the wedding, wreck the wedding. You must have your reasons or you wouldn't be sobbing. There there, poor thing, poor thing. You must just do what has to be done to stop yourself sobbing.

Exit. Enter LUCIAN.

LUCIAN: Where are Wulf and Sarah?

BROOK: Is everything alright?

LUCIAN: Yes, everything's fine! How could it be better? Your daughter is about to be married to a splendid young man she loves and who loves her.

BROOK: Things would be so much better, Lucian, if you and I could only talk from time to time.

LUCIAN: What do you mean?

BROOK: I must confess I am a selfish man, but I stand in need of God, like everyone else, and more than ever now on this day when I am supposed to be glad.

LUCIAN: Are you not glad? Do you not like Wulf? Do you not want him to marry your daughter?

BROOK: (*Screams.*) It is an abomination!

LUCIAN: What?

BROOK: Why do you never speak to me, Lucian? If you and I were friends now as we were once friends, I would be able to tell you. But as it is, what do I see before me, a man of the cloth, swaddled in faith.

LUCIAN: Wasn't I always?

BROOK: I have always fondly assumed that when your memory at last returned, if it ever did, and I doubted it would – but if it did, you would remember the things we endured, that there would be about you the look of a man who has suffered as I have suffered, that the lines in your face would be the same as mine, that we would talk about our dead friends, that we would be, in short, men of the same generation.

LUCIAN: That is not what has happened.

BROOK: But you did remember something! That made you walk the first time! I still cling to the hope that one day you will tell me!

LUCIAN: Oh that! That was not a memory! I am certain it was just a nightmare in the daytime.

BROOK: It was a memory! Otherwise you would not have walked! It gave you back your legs then, just as the memory of your religion has given you back you legs for good this time! Was that what you remembered before – your religion?

LUCIAN: No. No.

BROOK: What was it then?

LUCIAN: Something that conflicts with possibility.

BROOK: Tell me!

LUCIAN: No!

BROOK: Tell me!

He knocks him down.

LUCIAN: You are forgiven.

BROOK: It is now my intention, on this fateful day, to tell you
something I have never quite told you. I already know
what you remembered!

LUCIAN: How could you?

BROOK: Where did we get to last time? Ah yes. It is night
time, in the ruins. This is peacetime. The young baby
peace is still covered in its mother's blood. But certain of
the Germans are helping us and we are helping them with
the reconstruction, normal human relations are beginning
to spring up again, certain German nurses and nuns are
permitted to use our medical supplies to attend to civilians
sickening from starvation or wounded or in other ways
suffering. All this is excellent, I give my permission, and
you lead the work, you, the chaplain. You hold services
attended by both Germans and Englishmen – communion
– hymns rise out of the sky-roofed churches! One
particular woman, a young doctor, is always by your
side, an angel to the stricken, sweetness itself, a fresh
stream walking. In her eyes you could cast off the whole
experience, see quite a different past, history rewritten!
Ah but that beauty was too much for your war-stained
mind to bear. Like when Christopher carried God over
the river, she grew heavier and heavier, her purity and
grace a curse – too much light! How could we have known
how close you were to breaking, you who had carried
the entire regiment for four years – you yourself had no
inkling! In a kind of blasted graveyard you forced yourself
on her – and then – to silence her witness, beat her, to
death as you thought, left her there and continued on your
way – your way where? To Jerusalem? Your winding way,
the very longest way round to heaven. Then Lucian, by
a dark miracle, around the corner a bomb that had been
sleeping underground, one of ours, I imagine, that had
pierced the earth's crust without triggering its detonation,

went off – and lifted you into the wind. You were found unwounded, but knocked out. But since that day you have not remembered anything!

LUCIAN: Did she say I did it?

BROOK: She would not speak. She disappeared soon after. But you were lying very near her, with some of her possessions in your jacket pocket.

LUCIAN: Why have you not reminded me before?

BROOK: I tell you this story maybe once a year. Lucian, my old friend. I do not do it to cause you pain but in the hopes that it will all come back, and you and I will be friends again. Do not be afraid to remember. I will help you, as you helped me. I need you now just as much as I ever did in Africa or Italy or Normandy! It is all very well to die at a young age, in uniform, surrounded by ten thousand friends, but to drip like lard through a wicker frame, to perish like an old bird in an empty house left in its cage, with a daughter who does not love me, and and an old friend who does not remember!

LUCIAN: I beat her – nearly to death – a chaplain – ? That is not what I remember!

BROOK: By the end of today you will not remember anything I have said to you. You cannot hold onto the horror. I ought to speak it sweeter, but anything less than the kiss of truth would be useless to wake you.

LUCIAN: A woman I knew? That surprises me – that surprises me –

BROOK: Do you remember now?

LUCIAN: No!

BROOK: I know how you got like this! You are my mirror! It is all pride! It's the wicked one who whispers in your ear, you are not like them, no, to you fire is ice – forget them! Do you see? Evil is just amnesia!

LUCIAN: Well you have started something –

BROOK: What? Is it coming back?

LUCIAN: No – quite the opposite.

BROOK: Abandon the wedding!

LUCIAN: No I won't. I think it is right to continue as I am. It is expected that I shall perform the ceremony.

BROOK: I will tell them you are faking!

LUCIAN: If you wish to resist this wedding, oppose it openly. Myself I believe I must see it through in my own way. This is my plan. I think it is what Willow would have done.

Exit BROOK. Exit LUCIAN.

SCENE SEVEN

The church. Enter REGINALDA and RONALDO to their places. WULF sits near the altar. LUCIAN enters from the back. Enter CLARA. She sits next to REGINALDA. REGINALDA squirms away from her.

REGINALDA: Dear heaven, the wealth in here! No wonder no flaming angels have descended – they wouldn't be noticed among the bright little bags, the twinkling fingers, the aquamarine buttons, and the brilliant children! Ron, I hope you are taking this in, this celestial assembly we are sitting among.

RONALDO: Hush!

REGINALDA: Wafts of expensive breath –

RONALDO: Be quiet!

REGINALDA: Try to soak up some of this breeding. One thing about you, Ronaldo, I love you but you're bloody common.

RONALDO: Don't be so vulgar!

REGINALDA: I have no choice, since a holy father told me to enter in by the vulgate, that has been my calling. This vicar really does have an enormous organ.

RONALDO: I'm leaving!

REGINALDA: Hush, I'm only speaking in tongues.

RONALDO: You shouldn't have come!

REGINALDA: No one cares more about them! But do they realise this union has a two thirds chance of succeeding – and then – the odorous process of mutual maturation like two plums in a compost bin. At least they agree to part at death. Otherwise imagine the tedium of tender hauntings and jokey poltergeist fun everlasting. They are so inexperienced, the poor little peach slices – it should be forbidden for anyone to swear eternal fidelity who has not done so at least three times previously.

Organ music. Enter BROOK with SARAH. He is trembling. She breaks free and goes straight up to WULF.

What's the matter with him?

RONALDO: Who?

REGINALDA: The father. He's shaking like a washing machine.

RONALDO: He's full of emotion.

REGINALDA: You mean outright sweating terror! I'm worried for his Lordship. Perhaps the enemy have invaded. Dear God! See how he carries on regardless! Buckingham Palace is burning, but family must come first, God must be honoured, we shall tread the path of tradition to the bitter end!

RONALDO: Now concentrate on the matter in hand.

REGINALDA: There's nothing in mine, I swear. It's completely clean.

LUCIAN: Welcome everyone! Before we sing the first hymn, I would just like to say something. Something! There, I've said it. But there is much more than that, always far, far more to say than is ever said, it would take much talking to burn up that resource, an infinite amount, endless chatter, banter, discourse, endless description, confession! Or alternatively, we can say nothing, confess by silence the hopelessness of ever saying it all, ever really and truly even making the beginning of a beginning to remove that rockface with the toothpick of our tongue – give up before we even start because we know it can never be done, and we say nothing if we do not say everything, so best not to let the river begin. But here I am, talking and talking, as if to prove my point, like a cat of wind caught in a weather vane, chasing its tail as it strives to get back to the great wide onflowing!

WULF: We are anxious to marry! Please, get on with the wedding!

LUCIAN: Can anyone here offer any just cause or reason why this pair should be legally married? If not, then God have mercy on all of us.

WULF: That is not right!

LUCIAN: And half and head and how up tost? Craught in crack of cape, o hout? Hiff and wiff and piff and shish, aboft! Abaft! Haft! Hitch-half-hotch-oglotch-och-och

WULF: What on earth do you think you are?

LUCIAN: Where is the man who used me on that woman,
Took my left hand to clamp her throat, my right hand
To rip her dress, with my precise weight crushing
Her maiden bones, then, surging with my bloodstream,
Fled on my feet! This sleeve I bathe and sleep in,
This bed of flesh, was once a churchyard coven
To which came Satan when the moon was bleeding!
Horrible body, are you not ashamed!
No you are not, because you have forgotten!

BROOK: Now look here, Lucian –

LUCIAN: Silence! You people think that you are happy,
Entering through the porch in graceful pairs.
But let me tell you, under hell's white skies,
Seventy million people sit in silence!

Silence.

That was a truth too dark for you to think.
But every truth is brighter than the sun,
No matter how extravagantly black!
This is the only moment I enjoy,
You are all mine and that is all you know;
Your emptiness fulfills me utterly!

He doubles up in pain, then recovers.

What could I do, tell me, what could I do,
Having been made so beautiful and wise,
And then to be denied the utmost power?
You cannot tell me what you would have done,
For you were never wise or beautiful!
What was I meant to do with all my wisdom?
Who was enough like me to use my beauty?
For I am also the creator, I,
Anti-creator, and I named my creatures
Beautiful murder and sweet hate! I said
To misery, go forth and multiply,
Increase bereavement by the means of love!
I made you all, and though I may be lying,
Believe my lies, for I am Lucifer!
I do not fall, but anti-gravity
Makes me plunge upwards through eternity!

He rushes out.

WULF: Stop him!

REGINALDA: Is there another priest in the place?

BROOK: I am so sorry – please understand – the reverend is a veteran of the war – he suffered from shellshock – we thought he was cured. Please forgive him – he is still paying the price of our freedom! We will reconvene as soon as we can. Forgive him –

SARAH: He will marry us – let me talk to him –

REGINALDA: You will not find him now.

WULF: Do not speak to him!

SARAH: I must go after him.

REGINALDA: We will help you!

BROOK: Goodbye – goodbye everyone – I am so sorry – we will send out fresh invitations as soon as we can – goodbye auntie – goodbye Godfrey –

Exeunt.

SCENE EIGHT

In the woods. Enter REGINALDA and RONALDO.

REGINALDA: Clara! Clara! Lost her again! Clara!

RONALDO: It's not her we're looking for.

REGINALDA: She can't go on her own. What if she finds him? What will she say to him?

RONALDO: What will we say to him if we find him?

REGINALDA: I'll offer him a job. I'll say, come and be Satan in my circus.

RONALDO: Look – he's not over there –

REGINALDA: Then why are you going in that direction?

RONALDO: So as not to find him. We don't want any of that religion.

REGINALDA: You think Satan's religious?

RONALDO: Well he knows the Bible backwards.

REGINALDA: Are you trying to get promoted to clown again?

RONALDO: Some of your genius rubs off on me.

REGINALDA: That's not genius, it's foundation. Anyway I think religion is exactly what our circus needs, actually. We have so much faith, we only lack conviction.

RONALDO: I've had several convictions.

REGINALDA: Charges you mean, but they didn't stick, did they Ron? Because you've never actually done anything. Your epitaph could truly read, 'I was Nowhere Near the Place at the Time.' Officer.

RONALDO: I've been near all sorts of places.

REGINALDA: Approximation is all you have ever achieved. 'He Nearly Lived,' could be another epitaph of yours. I can imagine the dates – Almost Born, 1922, Very Nearly Died, 1968.

RONALDO: Well that suits me.

REGINALDA: Our friend is suffering in hell, waiting for rescue while you fester in putrid self-satisfaction.

RONALDO: I am only worried about what happens when we find him.

REGINALDA: Nothing that could possibly be worse than lingering out our duty of looking for him with inconsequential and irrelevant bickering.

RONALDO: You started it.

REGINALDA: No I didn't.

RONALDO: Yes you did.

REGINALDA: I did not.

RONALDO: You did.

REGINALDA: Didn't!

RONALDO: What does it matter anyway?

REGINALDA: That's my point – it doesn't!

RONALDO: What does then?

REGINALDA: Finding Lucian!

RONALDO: Well let's look for him then!

REGINALDA: Come on then!

RONALDO: Come on then!

Exeunt. Enter SARAH.

SARAH: Where is my old friend? I have neglected him. And
all this time he has been suffering such loneliness as even
I cannot imagine. I imagined that no one ever born could
be as lonely and empty and useless a piece of windblown
nothing as I was. And yet, by my side, all the time, was
a soul plunged seventy fathoms down under my floating
island. And I never took him seriously. I made it worse for
him, with my own weeping. I should have been looking for
him, looking for him. He was sinking, sinking, deeper and
deeper with every word or glance or blank look of mine. I
have been no help to him. Oh Lucian.

Exit. Re-enter RONALDO and REGINALDA.

REGINALDA: He's slipping away from us.

RONALDO: Every time we get close, he vanishes.

REGINALDA: He vanishes even when we're nowhere near.

RONALDO: Even when he's already invisible, he vanishes!

REGINALDA: And then vanishes a little bit more!

RONALDO: What chance have we got?

REGINALDA: We must seek in disguise. That way, he will feel
at ease, and, not recognising us, allow us to get close.

RONALDO: He fears everyone except strangers.

REGINALDA: But what if he is in disguise? What if he, by chance, chooses the same disguise as us?

RONALDO: But we have no other choice. Here – look – some clothes hanging on a washing line!

REGINALDA: That is just the kind of coincidence I dread.

RONALDO: We must not shy away from it.

REGINALDA: Put them on.

RONALDO: And creep off in opposite directions.

Exeunt different ways. Enter WULF and BROOK.

WULF: He is a missile aimed at my foundations. He cannot bear the fact of my existence, no matter how he may pretend, with priestly sweetness, the truth comes out! He does not want me to become something, to grow into a new being, since my smallest breath confirms his crime! As large as my love is for Sarah, so vast is my hate now for him!

BROOK: What will you do if you find him?

WULF: Sir – I will –

BROOK: Kill him?

WULF: Sir –

BROOK: Have no fear of the law, I can manage that. Act as if you and he were the only two men on earth. I think it is better for him to die than to remember.

Exit BROOK.

WULF: I must not think about my love's perfection,
Cause of all dawns, that rise in imitation
Of her, all stars that in the pebbled heavens
Change into eyes to view her lightfoot passing.
I must think only of my father's crime,

And what that means to the whole race of women,
And to myself, the everlasting victim,
Seen through the turned round telescope of him,
Tiny and weak. By this new revolution,
I will reverse the way of my conception.

Enter SARAH.

SARAH: Have you seen him?

WULF: No. I have not seen him. My love, we must not search together, that will halve our chances of finding him. You go and look over the other side of the house – or in the house, in the attic, or in the cellar maybe.

SARAH: I like looking with you.

WULF: I do not want you to.

SARAH: Why, don't you like me?

WULF: I like you violently. But I want to find this man, so that we can proceed to a proper wedding!

SARAH: You look under the shrubs, and I'll look up in the branches.

WULF: I insist – I command!

SARAH: I refuse. Are you angry with him?

WULF: No! Not in the slightest! But I am impatient. I am a half-married man, it is an uncomfortable feeling.

SARAH: We will not find him by rushing.

WULF: I know he is in this wood.

SARAH: Good! That's settled then.

WULF: But he might not be. Go to another place!

SARAH: I won't.

WULF: Get out of this wood, for God's sake!

SARAH: For God's sake get a grip on yourself!

WULF: Leave me alone!

SARAH: Alright I will. Forever.

Exit SARAH. WULF falls to his knees, clutching his head in his hands.

WULF: Oh God! Sorry – sorry – oh God –

Exit. Enter LUCIAN.

LUCIAN: Oh how the suffering of all shivering things
Warms me! Though ice is in the very veins
Of the stiff leaves, I burn with joy within
To think of fog-breath winter loitering
To mention their damnation to the dying.
Unchanging season of despair and gloom
Settled on hell, whose blank unloving sun
Fosters no growth – you fill my heart with chanting!
So I shall wander and survey my kingdom.

He walks a bit.

Stiff hare, I see by your obtruding eyes,
You were astonished in your former life,
Felt horror at the passing of each hour,
And could not grasp, as stones cannot grasp flies,
How all the folk kept up their talk of next year.
How voices from the garden next but one
Blent in contentment. And it stretched your ears.
You felt you held the horror of the world
All to yourself, foul treasure to be sure,
And not to share. And so your eyes bulged, hare,
And you grew legs for bounding once for all
Out of the world! But look, you are still here!
There is no flitting from my kingdom, hunched one!

He walks some more.

Frail blackbirds perched among the hips, not singing,
What is your trouble? Why so ruffled round,

Thinner than sticks beneath your puffed out plumes?
You were once workmen on a rooftop whistling,
But are not spared from hell by that position –
Both high and low are welcome in my kingdom!
Now I will tour my province, making plans
To spread forgetfulness like fern-spores wind-blown,
Rising from sleep, humanity's false friend!

Enter CLARA.

Well madam, I have done what I intended –
Blasted their putrid hearts! And in the mirror
Of their amazement I was meant to see
A picture of myself – by the damp firelight
Of their despair my spirit meant to gather
The pieces of itself, and put together
A person made of other people's tears.
But this does not yet seem to be beginning –
I am still waiting for a gleam of something –

She tries to speak but is unable.

You speak, but softly, in another country,
And I am deaf. But you shall be my Queen!
Together we shall be like war and famine,
From which no poverty escapes! Sit down!

She refuses to sit next to him.

Then I will do what I have done before –
Feast on your chirping soul, my wordless whore!

*He tries to rape her. She runs off. He follows, roaring. Enter
BROOK and WULF, meeting.*

BROOK: No sign of him?

WULF: Not yet!

BROOK: Hunt him, Wulf, hunt him!

*Exeunt. Re-enter LUCIAN to the aviary. The company acts out the
different kinds of birds, with different movements and cries.*

LUCIAN: This is the cage they call the aviary,
    Since it is full of birds, so they imagine,
    Rare birds from foreign airs whose character
    Shows in the rush and shuffle of their feathers.
    What we display with words they speak with feathers,
    Strutting their cresty plumes of bright invective
    And self-description, lifted on the pinions
    Of a pied noun. Like bishops and like kings,
    Their soul is in their robes, their life their rind.
    And to keep these encaged here in his garden
    Makes the Lord lie more lightly in his bedroom,
    Here are the claws of his imagination,
    Shrieks of his dreams, barred with curled iron and in
    Comparison to them he is not strange.
    But he is wrong! I know that you are demons,
    Feasting in secret on his inclinations;
    You are not birds! How did he get you in there,
    How did he think that if he kept you bordered,
    He would be free? So much atrocious power
    Crammed into one small cannon-space like powder,
    Must block him from all prophecies of freedom!
    Well I will let you out, and you can plague him
    In different ways; and all the rest of them!
    Fly out, high-soaring Mephistopheles,
    Reclaim the shaking kingdom of the trees,
    Where like hot planets your red cheeks did blaze!
    Go Moloch, make your awful shuffling way
    To peck at peace! Beelzebub, my pride,
    All burdened with the beauty of your eyes,
    Go, be the mirror in the human mind!
    Mammon, you golden spirit of the age,
    Cram love into a vault and lose the key!
    Belial, nightbird, with your cursing cry
    Make superstitious spirits fade away!

He lets out all the birds and enters the cage himself.

    Now I sit kingly on this stump that glows,
    Luminous moss where once the bark was clean,

Fungus offensive to the eyes and nose
Emerging phallic from the base, obscene,
Where slime-flux oozes and the bracket clings!
Here once the empire of an oak tree swayed,
Now in the void above, no redbreast sings,
In the clear air brave acorns were displayed,
Now I, more swift to kill than all disease,
Glorying in my evil, rule the scene,
And foul the place left by a prince of trees!

Enter SARAH.

SARAH: Lucian!

LUCIAN: Daughter of spite, you are most highly favoured!
Sit at my right hand here. My unkind kingdom
Will profit from your arrogance! Come closer!

SARAH: Lucian, you have let all the birds out! Oh my dear
friend, my dear friend!

She enters the aviary.

LUCIAN: You are quite pretty for a monster's daughter.
Come closer still, my sweet ship's cat, come closer.

SARAH: Oh what have we done to you?

LUCIAN: Nothing to what has been performed before!
And less than that to what will be again!
Well I have got you!

He bolts the door behind her.

SARAH: Got me, Lucian?

LUCIAN: Now I shall do what I have always done!

He tries to rape her. Enter REGINALDA and RONALDO.

REGINALDA: What's going on?

RONALDO: The birds are fighting!

REGINALDA: Weird birds, Ronaldo!

RONALDO: Not birds at all!

REGINALDA: That is the strangest kind of birds!

SARAH: Help me!

They enter the aviary and separate LUCIAN and SARAH.

God help him!

LUCIAN jumps out of the aviary and locks it behind him.

LUCIAN: Now burn there forever! I will fetch barrels of oil, and set light to them, and kill you with the smoke and flames!

He is about to exit. Enter WULF.

WULF: Sarah! Sarah!

SARAH: Wulf, stop him!

WULF: What did he do to you?

SARAH: It doesn't matter!

WULF: Your head is bleeding!

SARAH: It was an accident!

WULF: I understand! I know what he is!

He starts to strangle LUCIAN. Enter BROOK.

SARAH: Stop him!

WULF: He has helped himself, sir, to your daughter!

BROOK: Kill him.

REGINALDA: Only slightly! Please!

BROOK: Kill him! Kill him! Kill him!

WULF: Aaaaaggghhh! I cannot do it! I have not strength in my hands!

BROOK sees a rope lying on the ground.

BROOK: Here is a rope. Throw it over the tree.

SARAH: No!

RONALDO and REGINALDA start to squawk like birds. LUCIAN is bellowing with laughter. BROOK and WULF put a noose round his neck.

BROOK: Heave!

Enter CLARA. They stop.

CLARA: Let him go!

REGINALDA: She speaks!

CLARA: Let him go!

BROOK: Who are you to judge us? Go! Go! I evict you from my estate, you and all your circus! Leave! You have not brought me the slightest happiness! There is no bliss in tricks and freaks! The only joy is justice!

She removes her beard. He cries out and falls to his knees.

LUCIAN: Oh you! You!

CLARA: Do you remember me?

BROOK: This is the woman, Lucian!

LUCIAN: I am sorry! I am sorry! No – I am Lucifer!

BROOK: (*To CLARA.*) Say nothing! Do not speak! You have said enough! Leave my estate!

REGINALDA: She can't speak, can she dear?

CLARA: No.

REGINALDA: There, see.

CLARA: Lord Brook, I am staying right where I am.

BROOK: Wulf, this woman is a murderer!

WULF: She is my mother!

CLARA: Haha! Your court is collapsing!

BROOK: Will you believe this woman, Lucian, or will you believe me, your oldest friend? I am a Lord of England! She is an alien – a member of an enemy nation! What I tell you is true, what she tells you is dangerous lies! Drive her out of here!

SARAH: She has not said anything.

LUCIAN: Your Lordship, come with me, we will go down into the ground, and there we will live forever in the fire and the horror!

CLARA: Lucian! Lucian!

LUCIAN: My name is Lucifer! If you are an angel of heaven, fly far away from here, before I singe your feathers!

CLARA: Lucian! Lucian!

BROOK: Let us run away from her!

LUCIAN: Let her run away from us!

REGINALDA: You could run away from each other!

LUCIAN: Your Lordship, I will make you an equal in my kingdom! In hell we will be brothers!

CLARA: Lucian!

LUCIAN: If I failed to destroy you before, you will not be so fortunate this time!

CLARA: Destroy me then.

LUCIAN: I call forth the infinite thunder! I call forth the clamouring hellhounds! Let all the legions of the damned pour forth upon her! Azazeal, drag her down into the red-hot centre! Earth, open your rock lips and drink her like a poison river! There, where everything heavenly is mocked, she shall be despoiled, she shall curse her own name! Come, brother!

CLARA: Have you forgotten me? Am I so changed? Lucian!

LUCIAN: Silence! I am Lucifer, chiefest of those who suffer, cause of all torment, father of lies and wars, sea of amnesia!

CLARA: I remember you before you were the devil.

BROOK: She speaks pure evil, Lucifer!

SARAH: How dare you, father?

WULF: You shall not say this about my mother!

CLARA: I remember when you were an army chaplain. You were so sweet then. But something bad happened.

BROOK screams and lunges at her. WULF stops him, and holds him down.

LUCIAN: What are you accusing him of?

CLARA: Everything.

LUCIAN: I blast you to ether!

CLARA: And you, Lucian, he took your mind.

LUCIAN: I am dizzy, I don't understand.

CLARA: Lie down, lie down.

LUCIAN: I am falling in all directions.

He lies down.

WULF: Mother, where have you been?

CLARA: With the circus, in silence.

WULF: He is waking up!

LUCIAN wakes.

LUCIAN: Someone is moaning faintly in the graveyard as if bleeding to death. A newly dead child sobbing in its coffin? Or only a mourner? But who mourns here, in Berlin, all tears are finished. But look, look, there is someone there, like a scattering of leaves of all colours, orange, black, crimson, brown. I see who it is and what has been done. With her last breath she whispers a name and I run, thinking her dead. Then – nothing. There in the ruins of Berlin. My brother in arms. My commander. I did sin, yes, in loving her too much, and she was to have her child, we were to be married. And here he is. Forgive me, my son. I did not act as a man of God should have done. (*To BROOK.*) But how did you stick that guilt onto me? Dear God, you took your chance when I was lost. But tell me, my brother, what made you hate us so deeply? Was it Berlin?

SARAH: (*Looking at BROOK.*) What shall we do with him? He is the true Lucifer! How can he ever be forgiven? What could he do, crawl on his knees up every mountain in creation, offer himself up to ants to be slowly eaten? I cannot imagine anything – there is no horror, no hell foul enough for him!

RONALDO: You've never been to Brixton Prison.

REGINALDA: Ronaldo, we must fetch some officers to carry him away.

Exeunt RONALDO and REGINALDA; re-enter as WILLIAMS and BUCKLEY, or they just put on their masks.

WILLIAMS: Better come with us sir.

BUCKLEY: No monkey business.

WILLIAMS: He'll get ten years minimum.

SARAH puts the skull into BROOK's hand. Exeunt BUCKLEY and WILLIAMS with BROOK.

CLARA: Now we must finish this wedding.

Exeunt.

LAST SCENE

Outside Brixton Prison. Enter RONALDO *and* REGINALDA.

REGINALDA: Where's this prisoner? I should say this ex-prisoner. He's done his ten years.

RONALDO: They've sentenced him to ten minutes extra.

REGINALDA: For what?

RONALDO: For stretching credulity.

REGINALDA: Has anyone else come to meet him?

RONALDO: No fear.

REGINALDA: Here he comes.

Enter LORD BROOK, *dilapidated, in battered hat with suitcase.*

REGINALDA: Brooky! Over here! Have you got a job to go to? I have a suggestion, if your Lordship is willing. A vacancy has arisen in our troupe – the bearded woman. Will you take it, Lord Brook?

RONALDO: He is neither bearded nor a woman.

REGINALDA: Was Clara bearded? We thought so. Lord Brook?

BROOK: I do not know what you are talking about.

REGINALDA: Put on a dress and this beard, and come with us!

BROOK makes no move.

RONALDO: Please!

Exeunt BROOK and RONALDO.

REGINALDA: I am surprised, frankly, by the habits of the aristocracy. Who else would be so quick to embrace change? In this we see the real benefit of breeding. It is not a question of virtue – a coal merchant can be virtuous – it is a question of imagination. The nobility are tortured by their imagination! From their very earliest days they are fed with romantic notions and sentimental poetry that soften them without and within until they have no option but to be cruel, in self-defence against all us rough diamonds. And also we must pity the rich, forced by their wealth into upholding the present order in all its horror, against their better judgement. I propose a national year of silence in memory of the spirits of the rich and of the nobility. Unless they would all like to join my circus, in which case – jubilation!

Enter BROOK and RONALDO, BROOK in dress and beard.

No tears now, Clara!